MAXIMIZING YOUR POTENTIALS

Christy Lane

Copyright

Copyright © 2022 by Christy Lane

All rights reserved. No part of this book may be reproduced in any form or by any electronic or mechanical means, including information storage and retrieval systems, without permission in writing from the publisher, except by a reviewer who may quote brief passages in a review.

This book is a work of non-fiction. Any references to historical events, real people, or real places are used fictitiously. Other names, characters, places, and events are products of the author's imagination, and any resemblance to actual events or places or persons, living or dead, is entirely coincidental.

Published by Amazon

First edition, 2022

Table of Contents

Chapter One -Potentials and You 4
Chapter Two: Understanding Your Personal Strengths and Weaknesses 8
Chapter Three: Setting Clear Goals and Developing a Plan to Achieve Them ... 28
Chapter Four: Cultivating a Growth Mindset 38
Chapter Five: Building a Support System and Seeking Mentorship 41
Chapter Six: Time Management and Self-Discipline 46
Chapter Seven: Developing Strong Communication and Leadership Skills 50
Chapter Eight: Taking Care of Your Physical and Mental Health 54
About Maximizing Your Potentials 59

Chapter One - Potentials and You

Potential is the inherent ability or capacity for something to develop or be achieved. It is the possibility of achieving something in the future, based on a person's talents, abilities, and circumstances.

Everyone has the potential to achieve something, but the specific things that each person has the potential to achieve will vary based on their individual characteristics and circumstances. Some people may have the potential to excel in certain areas, such as sports, music, or academia, while others may have the potential to excel in different areas.

It is important to note that potential is not fixed and can be developed and expanded over time through effort, learning, and experience. Therefore, it is possible for anyone to maximize their potential and achieve success in their chosen field or pursuit, provided they are willing to work hard, learn, and persevere.

How do potentials manifest?

Potential can manifest in a variety of ways, depending on the specific talents, abilities, and circumstances of the individual. Some common ways in which potential may manifest include:

1. Natural abilities or talents: Some people may have a natural aptitude or talent for certain activities or subjects, which can help them excel in those areas.

2. Hard work and effort: Even if someone does not have a natural talent or aptitude for something, they can still achieve success through hard work and effort.

3. Learning and practice: Engaging in learning and practicing a skill or activity can help someone develop their potential and become proficient in that area.

4. Persistence and determination: Staying motivated and determined, even in the face of challenges or setbacks, can help someone reach their potential and achieve their goals.

5. Positive mindset: Adopting a positive mindset and believing in one's own abilities can help someone achieve their potential and overcome obstacles.

6. Support from others: Receiving support and encouragement from others, such as friends, family, or mentors, can also help someone reach their potential.

Ultimately, how potential manifests will depend on the unique combination of factors that each individual possesses.

The Importance of Maximizing Your Potentials

There are many reasons why it is important to maximize your potential. Here are five key points to consider:

1. Personal fulfillment: Maximizing your potential can help you feel more fulfilled and satisfied with your life, as you are able to achieve your goals and pursue your passions.

2. Career success: In many cases, maximizing your potential can lead to greater success in your career. By developing your skills and abilities, you may be able to advance in your field or pursue new opportunities.

3. Positive impact on others: By maximizing your potential, you may be able to make a positive impact on others, whether through your work, your contributions to your community, or your personal relationships.

4. Improved mental and physical health: Engaging in activities that help you maximize your potential can also have a positive impact on your mental and physical health. Pursuing your passions and goals can lead to increased happiness, satisfaction, and well-being.

5. Personal growth and development: Finally, maximizing your potential can lead to personal growth and development. As you work to achieve your goals and pursue your passions, you may learn new things about yourself and develop new skills and abilities. This can help you become a more well-rounded and self-aware person.

The Story of Sarah

Meet Sarah, a 25-year-old who has always been interested in art. Growing up, she spent most of her free time drawing and painting, and she always received positive feedback from her teachers and family members about her artistic abilities. However, Sarah never pursued her passion for art beyond a hobby, and instead decided to study business in college. After graduation, she landed a job at a marketing firm, where she has been working for the past two years.

Despite enjoying her job and being successful at it, Sarah has always felt like something was missing. She finds herself constantly thinking about art and feeling a sense of longing to pursue it more seriously. However, she has always been hesitant to take the leap, as she is worried about financial stability and the uncertain nature of a career in art.

Sarah has a lot of untapped potential in the artistic field, as she has a natural talent and a passion for it. However, she has not yet fully pursued this potential, as she has not taken the steps necessary to turn her hobby into a career. If Sarah were to take the leap and focus on maximizing her potential in the art world, she could potentially achieve great success and fulfillment in her career.

Do You Have Untapped Potentials?

It is possible that the you may have some similarities with Sarah in terms of having untapped potential. Like Sarah, you may have a natural talent or passion for something, but may not have fully pursued it due to various obstacles or fears. It is important for you to consider their own potential and whether they are maximizing it to the best of their ability.

Some questions you may want to ask themselves to determine if they have untapped potential include:

- What are my passions and interests?
- Do I have any natural talents or abilities that I have not fully developed?
- Have I been hesitant to pursue my passions or interests due to fear or other obstacles?
- Is there anything I am currently doing that is not fulfilling or meaningful to me, and could I be doing something else that would be more fulfilling?

By reflecting on these questions, you may be able to identify areas of untapped potential and take steps to maximize it. Just like Sarah, you has the potential to achieve success and fulfillment by pursuing their passions and talents.

Chapter Two: Understanding Your Personal Strengths and Weaknesses

There are many different types of strengths that a person may possess. Some common types of strengths include:

1. Intellectual strengths: These are strengths related to thinking, learning, and problem-solving, such as being a critical thinker, being good at analyzing data, or being skilled at problem-solving.

2. Physical strengths: These are strengths related to physical abilities, such as being physically fit, being agile, or having good hand-eye coordination.

3. Creative strengths: These are strengths related to creative thinking and expression, such as being artistic, being able to come up with innovative ideas, or being skilled at storytelling.

4. Interpersonal strengths: These are strengths related to relationships and communication, such as being a good listener, being able to persuade others, or being skilled at conflict resolution.

5. Leadership strengths: These are strengths related to leading and motivating others, such as being a good leader, being able to inspire others, or being skilled at managing projects.

6. Emotional strengths: These are strengths related to emotions and self-regulation, such as being able to manage stress effectively, being empathetic, or being resilient.

It is important to note that everyone has different strengths, and that it is normal to have a mix of different types of strengths.

On the other hand, weaknesses are areas where a person may struggle or need to work harder. Some common examples of weaknesses include:

1. Lack of knowledge or skills: A person may have a weakness in a particular subject or skill if they have not had the opportunity to learn or practice it.

2. Difficulty with organization: Some people may struggle with organization and time management, which can lead to disorganization and a lack of efficiency.

3. Poor communication skills: A person may have a weakness in communication if they struggle to express themselves clearly or if they have difficulty understanding others.

4. Lack of confidence: Some people may lack confidence in their abilities, which can hold them back from pursuing their goals or taking on new challenges.

5. Difficulty with problem-solving: Some people may struggle to come up with solutions to problems, or may have a hard time making decisions.

6. Poor physical fitness: A person may have a weakness in physical fitness if they struggle to maintain good health or if they have difficulty with physical activities.

It is important to note that weaknesses are not necessarily permanent, and that they can be improved upon through learning, practice, and effort.

What Makes Up Your Personality?

Strengths and weaknesses can have a significant impact on a person's personality and behavior. Here are five ways in which strengths and weaknesses can affect personality type:

1. Strengths can influence a person's confidence and self-esteem: A person's strengths can contribute to their confidence and self-esteem, as they are able to excel in areas that come naturally to them. This can lead to a more positive and self-assured personality.

2. Weaknesses can lead to insecurities and self-doubt: On the other hand, weaknesses can lead to insecurities and self-doubt, as a person may struggle with areas that do not come naturally to them. This can impact their personality and behavior, leading to a lack of confidence or a tendency to avoid certain tasks or challenges.

3. Strengths can contribute to a person's success: A person's strengths can also contribute to their success in various areas of life, such as their career or personal relationships. This can lead to a sense of accomplishment and pride, which can influence their personality and behavior.

4. Weaknesses can hold a person back: Conversely, weaknesses can hold a person back and prevent them from achieving their goals. This can lead to frustration and disappointment, which can impact their personality and behavior.

5. Strengths and weaknesses can both be developed: It is important to note that strengths and weaknesses are not fixed, and that they can be developed over time through learning, practice, and effort. By working to improve their

weaknesses and build upon their strengths, a person can positively impact their personality and behavior.

Overall, a person's strengths and weaknesses can have a significant influence on their personality and behavior, and it is important for individuals to be aware of their own strengths and weaknesses in order to maximize their potential and achieve success.

A Few Personality Types

There are many different personality types that can be identified, and each person has a unique combination of characteristics that make up their personality. Here are some examples of personality types:

- Extroverted: This type of personality is characterized by being outgoing, sociable, and assertive. Extroverted individuals tend to enjoy being around other people and may have a large social circle.

- Introverted: This type of personality is characterized by being more reserved, reflective, and inward-focused. Introverted individuals tend to prefer solitude and may have a smaller social circle.

- Sensing: This type of personality is characterized by being practical, realistic, and grounded in the present. Sensing individuals tend to focus on concrete facts and details, rather than abstract ideas or theories.

- Intuitive: This type of personality is characterized by being more imaginative, innovative, and abstract. Intuitive individuals tend to focus on the big picture and may be more open to new ideas and theories.

- Thinking: This type of personality is characterized by being logical, analytical, and objective. Thinking individuals tend to rely on reason and logic when making decisions, rather than emotion.

- Feeling: This type of personality is characterized by being more empathetic, compassionate, and emotional. Feeling individuals tend to rely on their emotions and values when making decisions.

- Judging: This type of personality is characterized by being organized, decisive, and planful. Judging individuals tend to like structure and may prefer to make decisions quickly.

- Perceiving: This type of personality is characterized by being more flexible, adaptable, and open-minded. Perceiving individuals tend to be more spontaneous and may prefer to keep their options open.

It is important to note that these are just a few examples of personality types, and that individuals can exhibit traits from multiple types. There is no one "right" personality type, and it is important for individuals to embrace their unique characteristics and strengths.

The Introvert

Introverts are individuals who tend to be more reserved, reflective, and inward-focused, and who may prefer solitude to being around other people. Here are some strengths and weaknesses that are commonly associated with introverts:

Strengths:

- Good listeners: Introverts tend to be good listeners and may be skilled at paying attention to others and understanding their perspective.

- Thoughtful and reflective: Introverts often have a rich inner life and may be more reflective and introspective than extroverts.

- Good at independent work: Introverts may be more self-motivated and able to work independently, without needing a lot of external support or guidance.

Weaknesses:

- May struggle with social situations: Introverts may struggle in social situations, especially if they are not familiar with the people or the setting. They may feel uncomfortable or overwhelmed in large groups or in unfamiliar environments.

- May have difficulty speaking up: Introverts may have difficulty speaking up or expressing their opinions in front of others, especially if they are not comfortable with public speaking or are not confident in their ideas.

- May be perceived as aloof or distant: Because introverts tend to be more reserved, they may be perceived as aloof or distant by others, which can make it more difficult for them to form relationships or build connections with others.

The Extrovert

Extroverts are individuals who tend to be more outgoing, sociable, and assertive, and who may enjoy being around other people. Here are some strengths and weaknesses that are commonly associated with extroverts:

Strengths:

- Good at socializing: Extroverts tend to be skilled at socializing and may be comfortable in a variety of social situations.

- Confident and assertive: Extroverts are often confident and assertive, and may be more comfortable speaking up and expressing their opinions.

- Good at networking: Extroverts may have a large social circle and may be skilled at building relationships and networking with others.

Weaknesses:

- May struggle with solitude: Extroverts may struggle with being alone or with having too much quiet time, and may feel restless or bored without social stimulation.

- May be perceived as overly confident: Because extroverts are often confident and assertive, they may be perceived as being overly confident or arrogant by others.

- May struggle with self-reflection: Extroverts may struggle with self-reflection and introspection, as they may be more focused on external stimuli and social interaction.

The Sensing Person

Sensing individuals are those who tend to be practical, realistic, and grounded in the present. They tend to focus on concrete facts and details, rather than abstract ideas or theories. Here are some strengths and weaknesses that are commonly associated with sensing personalities:

Strengths:

- Good at paying attention to detail: Sensing individuals tend to be good at paying attention to detail and may be skilled at tasks that require careful attention to detail.
- Practical and grounded: Sensing individuals tend to be practical and grounded, and may be able to approach problems and challenges in a logical, step-by-step manner.
- Good at following rules and procedures: Sensing individuals may be good at following rules and procedures, and may be reliable and dependable in their work and personal life.

Weaknesses:

- May struggle with abstract concepts: Sensing individuals may struggle with abstract concepts or ideas, and may have a hard time understanding or relating to things that are not concrete and tangible.
- May be resistant to change: Sensing individuals may be resistant to change, as they tend to prefer stability and routine, and may have a hard time adapting to new situations or ideas.
- May be perceived as too practical or unimaginative: Sensing individuals may be perceived as too practical or unimaginative by others, as they tend to focus on the concrete and the present rather than abstract ideas or theories.

The Sensing Person

Sensing individuals are those who tend to be practical, realistic, and grounded in the present. They tend to focus on concrete facts and details, rather than abstract ideas or theories. Here are some strengths and weaknesses that are commonly associated with sensing personalities:

Strengths:

- Good at paying attention to detail: Sensing individuals tend to be good at paying attention to detail and may be skilled at tasks that require careful attention to detail.

- Practical and grounded: Sensing individuals tend to be practical and grounded, and may be able to approach problems and challenges in a logical, step-by-step manner.

- Good at following rules and procedures: Sensing individuals may be good at following rules and procedures, and may be reliable and dependable in their work and personal life.

Weaknesses:

- May struggle with abstract concepts: Sensing individuals may struggle with abstract concepts or ideas, and may have a hard time understanding or relating to things that are not concrete and tangible.

- May be resistant to change: Sensing individuals may be resistant to change, as they tend to prefer stability and routine, and may have a hard time adapting to new situations or ideas.

- May be perceived as too practical or unimaginative: Sensing individuals may be perceived as too practical or unimaginative by others, as they tend to focus on the concrete and the present rather than abstract ideas or theories.

The Intuitive Person

Intuitive individuals are those who tend to be more imaginative, innovative, and abstract in their thinking and decision-making. They tend to focus on the big picture and may be more open to new ideas and theories. Here are some strengths and weaknesses that are commonly associated with intuitive personalities:

Strengths:

- Good at thinking outside the box: Intuitive individuals tend to be good at thinking outside the box and may be skilled at coming up with creative or innovative solutions to problems.

- Open to new ideas: Intuitive individuals may be open to new ideas and theories, and may be more receptive to unconventional or unconventional perspectives.

- Good at seeing patterns and connections: Intuitive individuals may be good at seeing patterns and connections that others might miss, and may be skilled at synthesizing complex information.

Weaknesses:

- May struggle with practical details: Intuitive individuals may struggle with practical details and may have a hard time focusing on the nuts and bolts of a task or project.

- May be perceived as too abstract or impractical: Intuitive individuals may be perceived as too abstract or impractical by others, as they tend to focus on the big picture and may not always consider the practical implications of their ideas.

- May struggle with making decisions: Intuitive individuals may struggle with making decisions, as they may have a hard time weighing the pros and cons of different options and may prefer to keep their options open.

The Thinking Person

Thinking individuals are those who tend to be logical, analytical, and objective in their thinking and decision-making. They tend to rely on reason and logic when making decisions, rather than emotion. Here are some strengths and weaknesses that are commonly associated with thinking personalities:

Strengths:

- Good at analyzing and evaluating information: Thinking individuals tend to be good at analyzing and evaluating information, and may be skilled at breaking down complex problems into smaller parts in order to find a solution.

- Rational and logical: Thinking individuals tend to be rational and logical in their thinking, and may be able to make decisions based on objective criteria rather than being swayed by emotions or personal biases.

- Good at problem-solving: Thinking individuals may be good at problem-solving, and may be able to come up with creative or innovative solutions to challenges.

Weaknesses:

- May struggle with empathy and emotional intelligence: Thinking individuals may struggle with empathy and emotional intelligence, and may have a hard time understanding or relating to the emotions of others.

- May be perceived as too detached or unemotional: Because thinking individuals tend to rely on reason and logic rather than emotion, they may be perceived as too detached or unemotional by others.

- May struggle with making decisions based on values or morals: Thinking individuals may struggle with making decisions based on values or morals, as they may rely more on logic and reason than on personal beliefs or principles.

The Feeling Person

Feeling individuals are those who tend to be more empathetic, compassionate, and emotional in their thinking and decision-making. They tend to rely on their emotions and values when making decisions, rather than logic and reason. Here are some strengths and weaknesses that are commonly associated with feeling personalities:

Strengths:

- Good at understanding and relating to the emotions of others: Feeling individuals tend to be good at understanding and relating to the emotions of others, and may be skilled at empathizing with others and providing emotional support.

- Good at making decisions based on values and morals: Feeling individuals may be good at making decisions based on their values and morals, and may be more attuned to ethical considerations when making choices.

- Good at building and maintaining relationships: Feeling individuals may be good at building and maintaining relationships, as they tend to be empathetic and compassionate, and may be skilled at creating a sense of connection with others.

Weaknesses:

- May struggle with being objective: Feeling individuals may struggle with being objective, as they tend to rely on their emotions and values when making decisions, rather than on logic and reason.

- May be perceived as too emotional or sensitive: Because feeling individuals tend to be more emotional and sensitive, they may be perceived as too emotional or sensitive by others, which can make it more difficult for them to assert themselves or make decisions.

- May struggle with confrontation: Feeling individuals may struggle with confrontation, as they may have a hard time dealing with negative emotions or conflicts

The Judging Person

Judging individuals are those who tend to be organized, decisive, and planful in their thinking and decision-making. They tend to like structure and may prefer to make decisions quickly. Here are some strengths and weaknesses that are commonly associated with judging personalities:

Strengths:

- Good at planning and organization: Judging individuals tend to be good at planning and organization, and may be skilled at creating systems and processes to help them stay on track and achieve their goals.

- Decisive and proactive: Judging individuals tend to be decisive and proactive, and may be able to make decisions quickly and efficiently.
- Good at setting and achieving goals: Judging individuals may be good at setting and achieving goals, as they tend to be organized and planful in their approach to tasks and projects.

Weaknesses:

- May be resistant to change: Judging individuals may be resistant to change, as they tend to prefer structure and routine, and may have a hard time adapting to new situations or ideas.
- May struggle with flexibility and adaptability: Because they tend to be organized and planful, judging individuals may struggle with flexibility and adaptability, and may have a hard time adapting to unexpected changes or challenges.
- May be perceived as inflexible or rigid: Because judging individuals tend to prefer structure and routine, they may be perceived as inflexible or rigid by others, which can make it more difficult for them to build relationships or work in collaborative environments.

The Perceiving Person

Perceiving individuals are those who tend to be more open, adaptable, and spontaneous in their thinking and decision-making. They tend to be more open to new experiences and may prefer to keep their options open. Here are some strengths and weaknesses that are commonly associated with perceiving personalities:

Strengths:

- Good at adapting to change: Perceiving individuals tend to be good at adapting to change, and may be more flexible and adaptable than those with a judging personality.

- Open to new experiences: Perceiving individuals tend to be open to new experiences and may be more receptive to new ideas and perspectives.

- Good at improvising: Perceiving individuals may be good at improvising and coming up with creative solutions to unexpected challenges or problems.

Weaknesses:

- May struggle with organization and planning: Perceiving individuals may struggle with organization and planning, as they tend to be more spontaneous and open to new experiences, and may have a harder time sticking to a schedule or routine.

- May be perceived as disorganized or unreliable: Because perceiving individuals tend to be more spontaneous and open to new experiences, they may be perceived as disorganized or unreliable by others, which can make it more difficult for them to build relationships or work in collaborative environments.

- May struggle with making decisions: Perceiving individuals may struggle with making decisions, as they tend to keep their options open and may have a hard time weighing the pros and cons of different options.

How to build up your strengths while improving on your weaknesses

Everyone has strengths and weaknesses, but how can you make the most of yours to get ahead in life? It might sound like a daunting task, but it doesn't have to be. There are plenty of simple strategies that you can use to identify and build upon your strengths while simultaneously working on improving your weaknesses. In this section, we'll discuss how to build up your strengths while taking steps to improve on your weaknesses. From recognizing where you excel to finding ways to challenge yourself, read on for our best tips on how to make the most out of what you possess.

Define your strengths and weaknesses

When it comes to professional and personal development, it's important to focus on both your strengths and weaknesses. By understanding and leveraging your strengths, you can set yourself apart from others and achieve success. At the same time, acknowledging and working on your weaknesses can help you become a more well-rounded individual and prevent you from running into future obstacles.

To get started, sit down and make a list of your strengths and weaknesses. Once you have a good understanding of what they are, you can begin brainstorming ways to improve upon your weaknesses while continuing to build up your strengths.

For example, let's say you're an introverted person who tends to freeze up in social situations. You might put "working on my social skills" as one of your goals. To help you achieve this goal, you could start by attending networking events or joining a Toastmasters club. However, don't forget to also focus on playing to your strengths. For instance, if you're good at writing, try using that skill to connect with others online or through articles/blogs.

Ultimately, the key is to find a balance between developing your strengths and weaknesses. By doing so, you'll become a more well-rounded individual who is better equipped to handle whatever life throws your way.

Set goals to improve upon your weaknesses

It is important to set goals for yourself that will help you improve upon your weaknesses. By doing this, you will be able to build up your strengths while also working on improving your weaknesses. This can be a difficult balance to maintain, but it is important to focus on both aspects in order to become the best version of yourself.

Some things that you can do in order to set goals that will help you improve upon your weaknesses include:

-Identify what your weaknesses are. This is the first and most important step in setting goals to improve upon them. If you are not aware of what your weaknesses are, then you will not be able to effectively set goals to improve them.

-Set specific and achievable goals. Once you have identified your weaknesses, it is important to set specific and achievable goals for yourself. These goals should challenge you and push you out of your comfort zone so that you can grow and progress.

-Create a plan of action. In order to achieve your goals, it is important to create a plan of action that outlines how you will go about achieving them. This plan should be specific and realistic so that you can stay on track and make progress towards improving your weaknesses.

-Measure your progress. It is also important to measure your progress as you work towards improving your weaknesses. This will help you see how far you have come and how much more work needs to be done in order to reach your goal.

Create a plan to build up your strengths

If you want to get better at something, it's important to first identify your strengths and weaknesses. Once you know what areas you need to work on, you can create a plan to improve upon your weaknesses while simultaneously building up your strengths.

Here are some tips for creating a plan to build up your strengths:

1. Set realistic goals. When setting goals, be realistic about what you can achieve given your current skills and knowledge. Trying to accomplish too much too quickly is likely to lead to frustration and disappointment.

2. Take small steps. Break down your goals into small, manageable steps that you can complete easily. This will help you stay focused and motivated as you work towards improving your skills.

3. Practice regularly. Repetition is key when it comes to learning new things or improving upon existing skills. Make time for regular practice sessions so that you can see consistent progress over time.

4. Get feedback from others. Ask trusted friends or family members for honest feedback on your strengths and weaknesses. This can be helpful in identifying areas where you need to focus your efforts in order to make the most progress possible.

5 Seek out opportunities to use your strengths. Whenever possible, look for opportunities to use your existing strengths in new ways or practice them in different settings. This will not only help you feel

more confident but also give you a chance to further develop your skills

Take action and monitor your progress

When it comes to personal development, it's important to focus on both your strengths and your weaknesses. However, you may find it more difficult to improve upon your weaknesses than to build up your strengths. This is why it's important to take action and monitor your progress.

Here are some tips for how to take action and monitor your progress:

1. Set realistic goals for yourself. Don't try to accomplish too much at once or you'll become overwhelmed and discouraged.

2. Create a plan of action. This will help you stay focused and on track.

3. Take small steps each day. Even if you only make a little bit of progress, it will add up over time.

4. Monitor your progress regularly. This will help you see how far you've come and keep you motivated to continue working towards your goals.

Make adjustments as needed

As you go about your journey to becoming the best version of yourself, it's important to keep in mind that everyone is different. What works for one person might not work for another. So, as you're working on building up your strengths and improving upon your weaknesses, make adjustments as needed.

If you find that you're struggling in a certain area, don't be afraid to change up your approach. Maybe you need to spend more time focusing on that particular weakness. Or maybe you need to try a different method altogether. Whatever the case may be, just remember to be flexible and willing to adjust as needed.

The most important thing is that you don't give up on yourself. Believe in yourself and your ability to improve, and eventually you will reach your goals.

Building up your strengths and improving on your weaknesses can be an incredibly rewarding process. It is a great way to build self-confidence, while also helping you become the best version of yourself. By focusing on areas where you excel, identifying opportunities for growth in other areas, and implementing strategies that support your development, you can make strides towards achieving personal success. With dedication and perseverance, this method will help set you up for success both now and into the future.

Chapter Three: Setting Clear Goals and Developing a Plan to Achieve Them

What are Goals?

Goals are defined as the specific outcomes or achievements that an individual or organization aims to accomplish over a certain period of time. Goals can be short-term or long-term, and can be specific to a particular area of an individual's life or a particular project or initiative. Goals can help provide direction, focus, and motivation, and can help individuals and organizations to stay on track and make progress towards achieving their desired outcomes.

Goals can be personal, such as improving one's health, advancing one's career, or learning a new skill. Goals can also be professional, such as increasing profits, expanding market share, or launching a new product. Goals can be specific, such as saving a certain amount of money or completing a specific project, or they can be more general, such as becoming more organized or improving communication skills.

Ultimately, goals are important because they help individuals and organizations to clarify their priorities, focus their efforts, and measure their progress towards achieving their desired outcomes. By setting clear goals and developing a plan to achieve them, individuals and organizations can increase their chances of success and maximize their potential.

Why You Should Set Clear Goals

Having clear goals and a plan can provide a number of benefits, including motivation, direction, and focus. Some specific benefits of having clear goals and a plan include:

- Motivation: Setting specific, challenging goals can provide motivation and inspiration to work towards achieving them. By setting goals, individuals can feel a sense of purpose and direction, which can help to increase their motivation and drive.

- Direction: Setting clear goals can help to provide direction and focus, as it allows individuals to know what they are working towards and how to prioritize their efforts. With a clear sense of direction, individuals can make better use of their time and resources and increase their chances of success.

- Focus: Having a plan to achieve your goals can help to keep you focused on your objectives, and can help you to stay on track and avoid distractions. By setting clear goals and a plan, you can stay focused on what is important and avoid wasting time or energy on activities that do not align with your goals.

- Increased productivity: By setting clear goals and a plan, individuals can be more productive, as they know what they need to do and when they need to do it. With a clear sense of direction and focus, individuals can work more efficiently and effectively, which can help them to achieve their goals faster and more effectively.

- Sense of accomplishment: Achieving your goals can provide a sense of accomplishment and satisfaction, which can boost your confidence and motivation to set new goals. By setting clear goals and a plan, you can take control of your life and make progress towards achieving the things that are most important to you.

How to Set Smart Goals

SMART goals are defined as specific, measurable, achievable, relevant, and time-bound goals that provide a clear and actionable plan for achieving a desired outcome. Setting SMART goals can help to provide direction, focus, and motivation, and can increase the chances of achieving success. Here are some tips for setting SMART goals:

- Make your goals specific: Be specific about what you want to achieve, and define your goals in clear and concrete terms. For example, instead of setting a goal to "exercise more," set a goal to "exercise for 30 minutes at least 3 times a week."

- Make your goals measurable: Make sure that you can measure your progress towards achieving your goals, so that you can track your progress and stay motivated. For example, instead of setting a goal to "improve your writing skills," set a goal to "write one 500-word article per week."

- Make your goals achievable: Make sure that your goals are realistic and achievable, given your current resources and constraints. Setting unrealistic goals can lead to frustration and disappointment, so be sure to set goals that you can realistically achieve.

- Make your goals relevant: Make sure that your goals are relevant to your long-term objectives and align with your values and priorities. This can help to ensure that you are motivated to achieve your goals, and can increase the chances of success.

- Make your goals time-bound: Set deadlines for achieving your goals, and make sure to allocate enough time to complete each task. This can help to provide a sense of urgency and motivate you to stay on track.

By setting SMART goals, you can increase your chances of success and maximize your potential.

Identify Your Goals and Priorities

An action plan is a detailed plan of action that outlines the specific steps and tasks that need to be completed in order to achieve a particular goal. Action plans can help to provide direction, focus, and motivation, and can help individuals to stay on track and make progress towards achieving their goals. Here are some tips for creating an action plan and setting deadlines:

- Break down your goal into smaller, more manageable steps: By breaking down your goal into smaller, more manageable steps, you can make it easier to focus on one task at a time and avoid feeling overwhelmed.

- Prioritize your tasks: Determine which tasks are most important and tackle those first. This can help you to stay focused and ensure that you are making progress towards achieving your goal.

- Set deadlines: Deadlines can help to provide a sense of urgency and motivate you to stay on track. Make sure to set realistic deadlines that allow you enough time to complete each task, but that also provide a sense of urgency.

- Make a schedule: Create a schedule that outlines when you will work on each task, and make sure to allocate enough time to complete each task. Having a schedule can help you to stay organized and focused, and can prevent you from feeling overwhelmed.

- Consider any potential obstacles or challenges: Think about any potential obstacles or challenges that you may face as you work towards your goal, and consider how you will overcome them. This can help you to stay on track and avoid setbacks.

- Review and adjust your plan as needed: As you work towards your goal, be sure to review your plan regularly and make any necessary adjustments. This can help you to stay on track and ensure that you are making progress towards achieving your goal

Tools and Resources for Setting Goals

Goal-setting tools and resources, such as a planner or goal-tracking app, can play a valuable role in helping individuals to set clear goals and develop a plan to achieve them. These tools and resources can provide a number of benefits, including:

- Structure and organization: Goal-setting tools and resources can provide structure and organization, which can help individuals to stay on track and focused on their goals. For example, a planner can help individuals to schedule their tasks and deadlines, and a goal-tracking app can help individuals to monitor their progress and adjust their plan as needed.

- Motivation and accountability: Goal-setting tools and resources can provide motivation and accountability, which can help individuals to stay motivated and committed to their goals. For example, a goal-tracking app can allow individuals to set reminders or notifications to help them stay on track, and can provide encouragement and feedback as they work towards their goals.

- Visibility and clarity: Goal-setting tools and resources can provide visibility and clarity, which can help individuals to understand their progress and identify areas for improvement. For example, a goal-tracking app can provide graphs or charts to help individuals visualize their progress, and can allow them to see what they have accomplished and what they still need to work on.

Ultimately, goal-setting tools and resources can play a valuable role in helping individuals to set clear goals and develop a plan to achieve them. By leveraging these tools and resources, individuals can increase their chances of success and maximize their potential.

There are many different planners and goal-tracking apps available, and the best one for you will depend on your specific needs and preferences. Here are a few examples of planners and goal-tracking apps that you may find useful:

- Planners:
    - Bullet Journal: A flexible and customizable planner that allows individuals to track their goals, tasks, and appointments in a simple and intuitive way.
    - Day One: A journaling app that allows individuals to track their goals, reflect on their progress, and document their experiences.
    - Asana: A project management tool that allows individuals to create and track tasks, set deadlines, and collaborate with team members.
- Goal-Tracking Apps:
    - Habitica: A gamified task management app that allows individuals to track their goals, habits, and daily tasks, and rewards them for making progress.

- Way of Life: A habit tracker that allows individuals to set and track goals, and provides insights and analytics to help individuals understand their progress.
- Streaks: A habit tracker that allows individuals to set and track goals, and provides reminders and notifications to help individuals stay on track.

These are just a few examples of planners and goal-tracking apps, and there are many others available that may be a good fit for your needs. It is important to choose a planner or goal-tracking app that works for you and meets your specific goals and needs.

Overcoming Obstacles and Staying on Track

Life is full of challenges and obstacles. We all face them at some point in our lives, but how we respond to them makes all the difference. It's easy to get overwhelmed by the challenges that come our way, but with a bit of preparation and understanding of what lies ahead, you can stay on track and reach your goals. We will discuss strategies for overcoming obstacles and staying on track despite the hurdles that may come your way. From setting achievable goals to monitoring progress and more, read on to learn how you can stay focused and motivated when faced with adversity.

Recognizing Your Obstacles

When it comes to overcoming obstacles, the first step is always recognizing what they are. Once you identify your obstacles, you can start brainstorming ways to overcome them.
Some common obstacles that people face include:

- -Lack of motivation
- -Procrastination
- -Unrealistic expectations
- -Perfectionism
- -Fear of failure

If you can't seem to get started on your goal or you keep putting it off, lack of motivation may be your obstacle. To overcome this, try breaking your goal down into smaller steps that you can accomplish easily. Set yourself a deadline and find someone who will hold you accountable.

Procrastination is another common obstacle. We all do it from time to time, but if it's preventing you from achieving your goals, it's a problem. Again, breaking your goal down into smaller steps can help. Set a schedule for yourself and stick to it. Make sure that you allow yourself some flexibility though - don't beat yourself up if you miss a day here or there. Just get back on track as soon as possible.

Are your expectations too high? If you're constantly setting yourself up for disappointment, it's time to reevaluate your goals. Make sure that they are realistic and achievable. If not, break them down into smaller steps so that you can see progress along the way. Perfectionism can be a real obstacle when trying to achieve anything in life. No one is

Here are three tips to help you stay focused.

1. Get rid of distractions. Turn off your phone, close the door to your office, whatever you need to do to minimize distractions and better focus on the task at hand.

2. Take breaks. Working non-stop is not only unrealistic, but it's also unhealthy both mentally and physically. Make sure to take regular breaks throughout the day to recharge and come back refreshed and ready to work.

3. Delegate and ask for help when needed. You don't have to do everything yourself! If there are tasks that someone else can handle, delegate them off your plate so you can focus on what's most important. And if you find yourself struggling, don't be afraid to ask for help from friends, family or professionals who can offer

Staying on Track

There will be times in your life when you feel like you're up against a wall. You've been working hard, but it feels like you're not getting anywhere. It's important to remember that everyone faces obstacles, and it's how you overcome them that counts.

Here are some tips for staying on track:

1. Believe in yourself
The first step to overcoming any obstacle is to believe in yourself. If you don't think you can do it, you won't be able to. Remember that you are capable of anything you set your mind to.
2. Stay positive
It's easy to get bogged down by negative thoughts, but it's important to stay positive. Every setback is an opportunity to learn and grow. Keep your head up and focus on the good.
3. Set realistic goals
One of the reasons people get discouraged is because their goals are unrealistic. If your goal is too big or too difficult, it can be hard to stay motivated. Break your goals down into smaller, more manageable pieces so that you can see progress along the way.

Overcoming Setbacks

It is important to remember that every goal worth achieving will have its share of obstacles. The key is to stay focused and not let these setbacks derail your progress.
One way to overcome obstacles is to develop a strong support network. Talk to your friends and family about your goals and ask

for their help in keeping you accountable. Additionally, seek out mentors who can offer guidance and advice when you encounter roadblocks.

It is also important to remember that setbacks are often only temporary. If you keep pushing forward, you will eventually reach your goal. So don't give up! Stay positive and keep moving towards your goal.

Achieving Your Goals

There is no one-size-fits-all answer to the question of how to achieve your goals. However, there are some general principles that can help you overcome obstacles and stay on track.

First, it is important to have a clear and specific goal in mind. Vague or general goals are more difficult to achieve than specific ones. Second, create a plan of action for how you will achieve your goal. This will help you stay focused and on track.

Third, be prepared for setbacks and obstacles. They are inevitable and part of the journey to achieving any goal. If you encounter an obstacle, don't give up – find a way around it or through it. Finally, persist and never give up on your goal. It may take longer than you initially thought, but if you keep working at it eventually you will achieve success.

Overcoming obstacles and staying on track with our goals can be a daunting task, but it is not impossible. With the right mindset, planning, and dedication we can all reach our goals. By taking small steps every day towards achieving what we want, breaking down our tasks into smaller chunks and getting support from family or friends if needed, we are more likely to succeed than if we try to do everything at once. It takes time and effort but in the end it is worth it!

Chapter Four: Cultivating a Growth Mindset

The concept of a growth mindset, popularized by psychologist Carol Dweck, refers to the belief that one's abilities and intelligence can be developed and improved over time through effort, learning, and persistence. This contrasts with a fixed mindset, which is the belief that one's abilities and intelligence are fixed and cannot be changed.

Having a growth mindset can provide numerous benefits, including increased resilience, learning, and success. In this chapter, we will explore the concept of a growth mindset and how it differs from a fixed mindset, and we will discuss strategies for cultivating a growth mindset in order to maximize your potential and achieve success.

II. Understanding a Growth Mindset
A growth mindset is characterized by a belief in one's ability to improve and learn, a willingness to take on challenges, and a focus on effort and progress. Those with a growth mindset view setbacks and challenges as opportunities for learning and growth, rather than as failures or limitations.
By contrast, those with a fixed mindset may view setbacks and challenges as threats to their intelligence or abilities, and may avoid taking on challenges or trying new things for fear of failure. This can lead to a lack of resilience and a reduced ability to learn and grow.

III. Developing a Growth Mindset
There are several strategies that individuals can use to cultivate a growth mindset and increase their resilience, learning, and success. Some strategies include:

Setting challenging but achievable goals: Setting challenging but achievable goals can help individuals to stretch their abilities and encourage growth. By setting goals that are too easy or too difficult, individuals may not be challenged enough to learn and grow.

Seeking feedback and learning from failure: Seeking feedback and learning from failure can help individuals to identify areas for improvement and to develop a growth mindset. By viewing feedback and failure as opportunities for learning, rather than as threats to their intelligence or abilities, individuals can develop a more resilient and flexible mindset.

Adopting a positive attitude: Adopting a positive attitude can help individuals to stay motivated and focused on their goals, and can increase their resilience and ability to learn and grow. By focusing on the potential for growth and learning, rather than dwelling on setbacks or failures, individuals can develop a more positive and growth-oriented mindset.

Practicing mindfulness and self-reflection: Practicing mindfulness and self-reflection can help individuals to become more aware of their thoughts and beliefs, and can provide an opportunity to challenge and change fixed mindset beliefs. By examining their thoughts and beliefs, individuals can develop a more growth-oriented mindset and increase their resilience and learning.

IV. The Impact of a Growth Mindset on Success
The impact of a growth mindset on success has been the subject of much research and discussion, and it is generally believed that a growth mindset can have a positive impact on success in various areas, including education, business, and sports. Here are a few ways in which a growth mindset can impact success:

- Education: Research has shown that individuals with a growth mindset are more likely to achieve academic success, as they are more likely to take on challenging coursework and persist in the face of setbacks. For example, a study of high school students found that those with a growth mindset were more likely to receive higher grades and to be more engaged in their studies.

- Business: In the business world, a growth mindset can lead to increased innovation, adaptability, and leadership. For example, studies have shown that individuals with a growth mindset are more likely to embrace change and new challenges, and are more likely to learn from their mistakes and seek feedback.

- Sports: In sports, a growth mindset can help athletes to improve their performance and achieve success. For example, research has shown that athletes with a growth mindset are more likely to train harder, seek feedback, and embrace challenges, which can lead to improved performance.

Overall, it is clear that a growth mindset can have a positive impact on success in various areas. By cultivating a growth mindset and focusing on learning, improvement, and resilience, individuals can increase their chances of success and maximize their potential.

Chapter Five: Building a Support System and Seeking Mentorship

Having a strong support system and seeking mentorship can be an important factor in achieving success and reaching one's potential. A support system can provide accountability, motivation, and guidance, and can help individuals to navigate challenges and setbacks. Seeking mentorship can provide access to knowledge, experience, and resources, and can help individuals to grow and develop in their personal and professional lives.

In this chapter, we will explore strategies for building a strong support system and seeking mentorship, and we will discuss the importance of maintaining and nurturing these relationships.

Building a Support System

Building a strong support system can be an important step towards achieving success and reaching one's potential. Some strategies for building a support system include:

- Identifying your needs: Identifying your needs can help you to understand what type of support you are looking for, and can help you to find individuals who can provide the support you need. For example, if you are looking for motivation and accountability, you may want to seek out a friend or colleague who is goal-oriented and reliable.

- Finding like-minded individuals: Surrounding yourself with like-minded individuals can provide a sense of community and belonging, and can help you to stay motivated and focused on your goals. For example, if you are working towards a specific goal, such as starting a business, you may want to seek out others who are also interested in entrepreneurship.

- Seeking out mentors and role models: Seeking out mentors and role models can provide valuable guidance and support, and can help you to learn from the experiences and insights of others. When seeking out a mentor or role model, it is important to identify your goals and values, and to look for individuals who align with these goals and values.

The role of friends, family, colleagues, and community in building a support system

Your support system can include a variety of individuals, including friends, family, colleagues, and members of your community. Each of these groups can provide different types of support and can play a valuable role in helping you to achieve your goals.

For example, friends and family can provide emotional support and encouragement, and can help you to stay motivated and focused on your goals. Colleagues can provide professional support and guidance, and can help you to navigate challenges and setbacks in your career. Members of your community, such as members of a club or organization, can provide a sense of belonging and can help you to connect with others who share your interests and goals.

Seeking Mentorship

Seeking mentorship can be a valuable way to access knowledge, experience, and resources, and can help individuals to grow and develop in their personal and professional lives. Some benefits of seeking mentorship include:

- Access to knowledge and experience: Mentors can provide valuable knowledge and experience that can help individuals to learn and grow. By seeking out mentors who have expertise in a particular field or area of interest, individuals can gain valuable insights and guidance that can help them to achieve their goals.

- Networking opportunities: Mentors can provide valuable networking opportunities and can introduce individuals to other professionals or resources that can help them to achieve their goals. By building relationships with mentors, individuals can expand their professional network and increase their chances of success.

- Personal and professional development: Mentorship can provide a supportive and encouraging environment for personal and professional development. Mentors can provide guidance, support, and feedback that can help individuals to identify and work towards their goals, and can help them to overcome challenges and setbacks.

When seeking out a mentor, it is important to identify your goals and values, and to look for individuals who align with these goals and values. Some strategies for finding and approaching potential mentors include:

- Identifying your goals and values: Identifying your goals and values can help you to determine what you are looking for in a mentor, and can help you to find individuals who can support and guide you in achieving these goals.

- Researching potential mentors: Researching potential mentors can help you to identify individuals who have the knowledge, experience, and expertise that you are looking for. This may involve looking for mentors within your field or industry, or seeking out individuals who have achieved success in areas that you are interested in.

- Preparing a pitch: Preparing a pitch can help you to clearly articulate your goals and interests, and can help you to convince potential mentors that you are a good fit for their mentorship. This may involve preparing a short summary of your goals and interests, and explaining how a mentorship relationship would be beneficial to you.

The role of mentorship in personal and professional development

Mentorship can play a valuable role in personal and professional development, and can help individuals to identify and work towards their goals. By seeking out mentors who have expertise in a particular field or area of interest, individuals can gain valuable insights and guidance that can help them to achieve their goals. Mentorship can also provide a supportive and encouraging environment for personal and professional growth, and can help individuals to overcome challenges and setbacks.

Maintaining and Nurturing Your Support System and Mentorship Relationships

Maintaining and nurturing your support system and mentorship relationships can be an important step towards achieving success and reaching your potential. Some strategies for maintaining and nurturing these relationships include:

- Setting clear expectations: Setting clear expectations can help to ensure that your support system and mentorship relationships are productive and beneficial. This may include setting goals or objectives for the relationship, identifying how you will communicate and meet, and establishing boundaries.
- Being responsive and proactive: Being responsive and proactive can help to maintain and nurture your support

system and mentorship relationships. This may include following up on tasks and commitments, seeking feedback and support when needed, and offering support and appreciation to others in your support system or mentorship relationships.

- Offering support and appreciation: Offering support and appreciation can help to strengthen your support system and mentorship relationships. This may include expressing gratitude, offering help or resources when needed, and being there for others when they need support.

- The importance of communication and feedback: Communication and feedback are essential for maintaining and nurturing your support system and mentorship relationships. This may include regularly checking in with your support system or mentors, providing constructive feedback, and being open and honest about your needs and expectations.

In conclusion, building a strong support system and seeking mentorship can be an important factor in achieving success and reaching your potential. By cultivating and nurturing these relationships, you can gain valuable knowledge, experience, and support, and can increase your chances of success. Remember to set clear expectations, be responsive and proactive, and offer support and appreciation to those in your support system and mentorship relationships, and to prioritize communication and feedback in order to strengthen and maintain these relationships.

Chapter Six: Time Management and Self-Discipline

Effective time management and self-discipline are essential skills for achieving success and reaching one's potential. Good time management and self-discipline can help individuals to increase their productivity, reduce their stress, and improve their performance. In this chapter, we will explore strategies for managing time effectively, cultivating self-discipline, and overcoming procrastination.

Time Management Techniques

Effective time management can help individuals to get more done in less time, and can reduce stress and improve performance. Some strategies for managing time effectively include:

- Setting priorities: Setting priorities can help individuals to focus on the most important tasks and to allocate their time accordingly. By identifying the tasks that are most important and urgent, individuals can prioritize their time and ensure that they are using their time effectively.

- Creating a schedule: Creating a schedule can help individuals to plan their time and to allocate their resources effectively. This may involve creating a daily, weekly, or monthly schedule, and breaking tasks down into smaller, manageable chunks.

- Using tools and resources: Tools and resources, such as a planner, a to-do list, or a time-tracking app, can help individuals to manage their time effectively. These tools can help individuals to track their time, set reminders, and stay organized, which can increase productivity and reduce stress.

Self-Discipline Strategies

Self-discipline is the ability to control one's thoughts, feelings, and actions, and is essential for achieving success and reaching one's potential. Some strategies for cultivating self-discipline include:

- Setting goals: Setting goals can help individuals to focus their efforts and to stay motivated. By setting clear, specific, and achievable goals, individuals can establish a sense of purpose and direction, and can work towards achieving their goals with self-discipline.

- Establishing routines: Establishing routines can help individuals to develop self-discipline and to manage their time effectively. This may involve setting aside specific times for tasks, such as studying or exercising, and establishing consistent habits and patterns.

- Using positive reinforcement: Using positive reinforcement can help individuals to cultivate self-discipline by rewarding themselves for meeting their goals and staying on track. This may involve setting rewards or incentives, such as treating oneself to a favorite activity or food, or celebrating accomplishments.

- Mindfulness and self-awareness: Mindfulness and self-awareness can help individuals to develop self-discipline by increasing their awareness of their thoughts, feelings, and actions. By paying attention to their own behavior and choices, individuals can better understand their strengths and weaknesses, and can work towards cultivating self-discipline.

- Setting boundaries and managing distractions: Setting boundaries and managing distractions can help individuals to maintain self-discipline and to stay focused on their goals. This may involve setting limits on the amount of time spent on distracting activities, such as social media or television, and establishing boundaries around the use of technology

IV. Overcoming Procrastination

Procrastination is a common challenge that many people face, and it can be a major obstacle to achieving success and reaching one's potential. Procrastination is the tendency to delay or postpone tasks, and it can be caused by a variety of factors, including fear of failure, lack of motivation, and lack of clarity around goals or tasks. If left unchecked, procrastination can lead to increased stress, decreased productivity, and feelings of frustration and disappointment.

However, it is possible to overcome procrastination and to develop more productive and effective habits. To overcome procrastination, it is important to identify the root cause of the problem and to address any underlying issues. This may involve exploring one's own thoughts and feelings, and identifying any negative thought patterns or behaviors that are contributing to procrastination.

Identify the root cause of procrastination: Identifying the root cause of procrastination can help individuals to understand why they are procrastinating and to address the underlying issues. This may involve exploring one's own thoughts and feelings, and identifying any negative thought patterns or behaviors that are contributing to procrastination.

Set realistic goals: Setting realistic goals can help individuals to stay motivated and to avoid feeling overwhelmed. By setting goals that are specific, achievable, and measurable, individuals can break tasks down into smaller, manageable steps, and can stay on track towards achieving their goals.

Use positive reinforcement and accountability: Using positive reinforcement and accountability can help individuals to overcome procrastination and to stay motivated. This may involve setting rewards or incentives for meeting goals, or seeking support and accountability from friends or colleagues.

Effective time management and self-discipline are essential skills for achieving success and reaching one's potential. By cultivating these skills, individuals can increase their productivity, reduce their stress, and improve their performance. To maximize your potential and achieve your goals, it is important to set priorities, create a schedule, and cultivate self-discipline, and to overcome procrastination by identifying the root cause, setting realistic goals, and using positive reinforcement and accountability.

Chapter Seven: Developing Strong Communication and Leadership Skills

Strong communication and leadership skills are essential for achieving success and reaching one's potential. Effective communication and leadership can help individuals to build relationships, influence others, and achieve results. In this chapter, we will explore strategies for effective communication, developing leadership skills, and building and leading effective teams.

Communication Techniques

Effective communication is the foundation of strong relationships, and is essential for achieving success and reaching one's potential. Some strategies for effective communication include:

- Active listening: Active listening involves fully engaging with the speaker, and showing genuine interest in what they have to say. This involves paying attention, asking clarifying questions, and avoiding distractions.

- Clear and concise language: Using clear and concise language can help individuals to communicate effectively and to avoid misunderstandings. This may involve using simple, straightforward language, and avoiding jargon or technical terms.

- Nonverbal cues: Nonverbal cues, such as body language, facial expressions, and tone of voice, can also play a role in effective communication. By paying attention to these cues, individuals can better understand the message being conveyed and can more effectively convey their own message.

- Empathy and emotional intelligence: Empathy and emotional intelligence can help individuals to better understand the feelings and perspectives of others, and can improve communication and relationships. By practicing empathy and emotional intelligence, individuals can better connect with others and can more effectively communicate their thoughts and feelings.

- Handling difficult conversations and conflicts: Difficult conversations and conflicts can be challenging, but they are a normal part of life. To handle these situations effectively, it can be helpful to stay calm, listen actively, and try to find common ground. It may also be helpful to seek support and guidance from others, such as a mentor or a counselor.

Leadership Skills

Leadership involves inspiring and guiding others towards a common goal, and is essential for achieving success and reaching one's potential. Some characteristics of effective leaders include:

- Vision: Effective leaders have a clear vision of what they want to achieve, and can inspire and motivate others to work towards that vision.

- Integrity: Effective leaders are honest and trustworthy, and are committed to doing the right thing.

- Teamwork: Effective leaders value teamwork and collaboration, and can bring people together to achieve a common goal.

To develop leadership skills, individuals can:

- Set goals: Setting goals can help individuals to focus their efforts and to stay motivated. By setting clear, specific, and achievable goals, individuals can establish a sense of purpose and direction, and can work towards achieving their goals with leadership.

- Lead by example: Leading by example involves setting a positive example for others to follow. This may involve demonstrating integrity, honesty, and a strong work ethic, and being open to feedback and learning.

- Empower others: Empowering others involves giving others the tools and resources they need to succeed, and helping them to develop their own skills and abilities. This may involve providing support, encouragement, and guidance, and fostering a culture of continuous learning.

- Adaptability and continuous learning: Effective leaders are adaptable and are committed to continuous learning. By being open to change and new ideas, and by staying current with developments in their field, leaders can stay ahead of the curve and lead their team to success.

Team Building

Teamwork is essential for achieving success and reaching one's potential, and effective team building can help individuals to work together effectively towards a common goal. Some strategies for building and leading effective teams include:

- Setting clear goals: Setting clear goals is important for helping team members to focus their efforts and to stay motivated. By setting specific, measurable, achievable, relevant, and time-bound (SMART) goals, leaders can ensure that team members have a clear understanding of what is expected of them, and can work towards achieving those goals with a sense of purpose and direction.

- Fostering collaboration: Fostering collaboration involves promoting open communication, shared decision-making, and a sense of shared responsibility among team members. This can help to build trust and to encourage team members to work together towards a common goal.

- Promoting diversity: Promoting diversity in a team can bring a range of perspectives, skills, and experiences to the table, and can help to improve problem-solving and decision-making. By valuing diversity and inclusivity, leaders can create a positive and supportive team culture.

- Managing conflicts: Conflicts are a normal part of life, and can arise in any team. To manage conflicts effectively, it is important to stay calm, listen actively, and try to find common ground. It may also be helpful to seek support and guidance from others, such as a mentor or a mediator.

In conclusion, strong communication and leadership skills are essential for achieving success and reaching one's potential. By cultivating these skills, individuals can build relationships, influence others, and achieve results. To maximize your potential and achieve your goals, it is important to develop effective communication skills, leadership skills, and teamwork, and to build and lead effective teams.

Chapter Eight: Taking Care of Your Physical and Mental Health

Physical and mental health are essential for achieving success and reaching one's potential. Maintaining good physical and mental health requires self-care, or the intentional practice of taking care of oneself. In this chapter, we will explore the importance of physical and mental health, and strategies for maintaining these aspects of well-being through self-care.

Physical Health

Physical health is essential for overall well-being, and is important for maintaining the energy and vitality needed to achieve success and reach one's potential. Some strategies for maintaining physical health include:

- Exercise and nutrition: Exercise and nutrition are essential for maintaining physical health. Regular physical activity helps to improve cardiovascular health, reduce the risk of chronic diseases, and improve overall well-being. A healthy diet, rich in fruits, vegetables, and other nutrients, can also help to support physical health.

- Staying active and eating a healthy diet: Staying active and eating a healthy diet can be challenging, but there are strategies that can help. Setting goals, such as walking a certain number of steps each day or incorporating physical activity into daily routines, can help to increase physical activity. Similarly, setting healthy eating habits, such as eating regular meals, planning ahead, and avoiding unhealthy snacks, can help to maintain a healthy diet.

- Sleep: Sleep is essential for physical health, and can help to improve energy, mood, and overall well-being. To get enough rest, it can be helpful to establish a consistent sleep schedule, create a relaxing bedtime routine, and avoid screens and other distractions before bed.

Mental Health

Mental health is an essential aspect of overall well-being, and is important for maintaining the emotional and psychological well-being needed to achieve success and reach one's potential. Some common mental health challenges include stress, anxiety, and depression. To maintain mental health, it can be helpful to:

- Seek support: Seeking support, whether through therapy, counseling, or support groups, can be an important step in maintaining mental health. Support from others can help to reduce feelings of isolation and can provide a sense of connection and belonging.

- Practice relaxation techniques: Relaxation techniques, such as deep breathing, meditation, or yoga, can help to reduce stress and improve mental health. These techniques can be practiced at home or in a group setting, and can be a helpful way to cope with stress and maintain mental well-being.

- Set boundaries: Setting boundaries is important for maintaining mental health and well-being. This may involve setting limits on work or other commitments, or establishing clear boundaries around the use of technology. By setting boundaries, individuals can protect their time and energy, and can better manage stress and other demands.

Self-Care

Self-care is the intentional practice of taking care of oneself, and is essential for maintaining physical and mental health. Some strategies for practicing self-care include:

- Setting aside time for rest and relaxation: Taking time to rest and relax is important for maintaining physical and mental health. This may involve setting aside time for activities that bring joy and fulfillment, such as hobbies or leisure activities, or simply taking time to rest and recharge.

- Engaging in activities that bring joy and fulfillment: Engaging in activities that bring joy and fulfillment can help to improve mental health and well-being. This may involve hobbies, leisure activities or other activities that bring a sense of purpose or meaning.

- Seeking support from others: Seeking support from others, such as friends, family, or a support group, can be an important aspect of self-care. Support from others can provide a sense of connection and belonging, and can help to reduce feelings of isolation.

In conclusion, physical and mental health are essential for achieving success and reaching one's potential. Maintaining these aspects of well-being requires self-care, or the intentional practice of taking care of oneself. By prioritizing physical and mental health, and by practicing self-care, individuals can maximize their potential and achieve their goals.

Chapter Nine: Continuing to Learn and Grow Throughout Your Life

I. Introduction

Lifelong learning and personal growth are essential for achieving success and reaching one's potential. In an ever-changing world, it is important to stay current and relevant by continuing to learn and grow. In this chapter, we will explore the benefits of lifelong learning and personal growth, and strategies for continuing to learn and grow throughout your life.

II. Lifelong Learning

Lifelong learning is the process of continuing to learn and grow throughout one's life. Lifelong learning can bring a range of benefits, including increased knowledge, skills, and adaptability. Some strategies for continuing to learn and grow include:

- Setting learning goals: Setting learning goals is an important step in continuing to learn and grow. Learning goals should be specific, measurable, achievable, relevant, and time-bound (SMART), and should reflect your interests and career goals.

- Seeking new experiences: Seeking new experiences, such as taking on new challenges or trying new activities, can help to stimulate learning and growth. By stepping outside of your comfort zone and exposing yourself to new ideas and experiences, you can broaden your horizons and expand your knowledge and skills.

- Seeking out opportunities for growth: There are many opportunities for learning and growth, whether through formal education, professional development, or personal growth. By seeking out these opportunities, you can continue to learn and grow throughout your life.

- Staying motivated and engaged: Staying motivated and engaged in learning can be challenging, but there are strategies that can help. Finding a sense of purpose and meaning in what you learn, and seeking support from others, can help to keep you motivated and engaged.

III. Personal Growth

Personal growth is the process of developing and improving oneself, both personally and professionally. Personal growth can bring a range of benefits, including increased self-awareness, self-confidence, and self-fulfillment. Some strategies for personal growth include:

- Setting personal goals: Setting personal goals is an important step in personal growth. Personal goals should be specific, measurable, achievable, relevant, and time-bound (SMART), and should reflect your values and aspirations.

- Seeking feedback and self-reflection: Seeking feedback and engaging in self-reflection can help to identify areas for improvement and to track progress towards your goals. By regularly seeking feedback from others and engaging in self-reflection, you can gain insight into your strengths and weaknesses, and can set goals for growth.

- Seeking support from others: Seeking support from others, such as friends, family, or a mentor, can be an important aspect of personal growth. Support from others can provide encouragement, guidance, and a sense of connection and belonging.

- Staying motivated and engaged: Staying motivated and engaged in personal growth can be challenging, but there are strategies that can help. Finding a sense of purpose and meaning in what you do, and seeking support from others, can help to keep you motivated and engaged.

IV. Conclusion

In conclusion, lifelong learning and personal growth are essential for achieving success and reaching one's potential. By continuing to learn and grow throughout your life, you can stay current and relevant, and can achieve your goals and reach your full potential. To continue to learn and grow, it is important to set goals, seek new experiences, seek out opportunities for growth, and stay motivated and engaged.

About Maximizing Your Potentials

"Maximizing Your Potential" is a comprehensive guide to reaching your full potential and achieving success in all areas of your life. The book explores a range of key topics, including goal-setting, growth mindset, building a support system, time management and self-discipline, communication and leadership skills, physical and mental health, and lifelong learning and personal growth.

Throughout the book, readers will learn valuable strategies and techniques for maximizing their potential and achieving their goals. The book begins by exploring the concept of potential and how it manifests in different individuals. It then delves into the importance of setting clear goals and developing a plan to achieve them, including tips for creating an action plan and setting deadlines.

One key theme of the book is the cultivation of a growth mindset, which is the belief that one's abilities and intelligence can be developed through effort and learning. The book explores the impact of a growth mindset on success, and provides strategies for cultivating a growth mindset in oneself and others.

Another important aspect of the book is the importance of building a support system and seeking mentorship. The book discusses the benefits of having a strong support system and the role of mentorship in personal and professional growth. It also provides tips for building a support system and seeking out mentors.

The book also covers important skills such as time management and self-discipline, which are essential for staying focused and motivated in achieving one's goals. The book provides strategies for improving these skills, including tips for overcoming procrastination and setting boundaries.

In addition to these practical skills, the book also focuses on the importance of taking care of one's physical and mental health. It discusses the impact of physical and mental health on overall well-being, and provides strategies for maintaining these aspects of health through self-care.

Finally, the book emphasizes the importance of continuing to learn and grow throughout one's life. It discusses the benefits of lifelong learning and personal growth, and provides strategies for staying motivated and engaged in these processes.

Overall, "Maximizing Your Potential" is a valuable resource for anyone looking to achieve success and reach their full potential. It provides practical strategies and techniques for setting goals, cultivating a growth mindset, building a support system, improving time management and self-discipline, and taking care of physical and mental health. By following the advice in this book, readers can maximize their potential and achieve their goals

www.ingramcontent.com/pod-product-compliance
Lightning Source LLC
Chambersburg PA
CBHW050309220526
45465CB00005B/1921